# We Shall Overcome

by Chanelle Peters

PEARSON

Scott
Foresman

Editorial Offices: Glenview, Illinois • Parsippany, New Jersey • New York, New York
Sales Offices: Needham, Massachusetts • Duluth, Georgia • Glenview, Illinois
Coppell, Texas • Ontario, California • Mesa, Arizona

ISBN: 0-328-13487-2

## A Fight for Freedom

For hundreds of years, **generations** of African Americans have struggled to be treated as equals in the United States. Many were forced to come to the United States as enslaved people. Over time, many Americans saw this was wrong and fought hard to end slavery. Even after slavery was over, though, the fight for equality continued.

The first Africans brought to the United States had been captured and taken from their homelands in Africa. They came to the United States by boat. Once in the United States, most Africans were sold and forced to work on large farms called plantations.

Enslaved people from Africa work on a plantation.

3

AM I NOT A MAN AND A

UAW SAYS
BLACK and
WHITE
UNITE...
FOR
WHAT'S
RIGHT!

4

The captured Africans resisted being enslaved. Some Africans would fight members of the ship's crew on the way to the United States. Others would jump into the ocean. Some Africans would wait until they were in the United States to fight back. Some ran away from the plantation owners. Others pretended to be sick. Some simply refused to work. Sadly, it was going to take a much larger effort to put an end to slavery in the United States.

In the early 1800s **numerous** African and European Americans joined together to fight against slavery. Their goal was to abolish, or end, slavery. They became known as abolitionists. Many abolitionists formed groups, held meetings and conferences, refused to buy products made by enslaved people, and gave speeches about ending slavery. However, the struggle was deeper and more personal for African Americans. They wanted to have equal rights in the United States.

African Americans wanted their freedom.

5

## The Abolitionist Movement

William Lloyd Garrison

In 1829 a people's abolitionist movement began with the writings of David Walker. Walker's father was an enslaved man and his mother was a free African American woman. Walker was interested in the fact that not all African Americans were enslaved. Walker's writing told enslaved people to use force when rebelling, or fighting back, against their masters.

William Lloyd Garrison was a European American abolitionist who did not agree with Walker's idea of using violence to help end slavery. From 1831 to 1865, Garrison published a newspaper called *The Liberator* and in it asked abolitionists to use nonviolent actions to change peoples' minds about slavery.

Another abolitionist who believed in nonviolence was Frederick Douglass. He had been enslaved in Maryland before escaping to freedom. Douglass spent most of his life giving speeches about equality and the end of slavery. Douglass also published a book in 1845 about his life as an enslaved man. It was called *Narrative of the Life of Frederick Douglass, an American Slave, Written by Himself.*

Frederick Douglass

Women also played an important role in the abolitionist movement. They spoke out against slavery through public speaking and writing. Many women escaped slavery themselves and went on to help others escape to freedom.

In 1831 Maria Stewart began writing and making speeches about ending slavery and making the lives of African American people better. Stewart was African American and the first American woman ever to speak about political issues in public. She strongly believed in equal rights not just for African Americans but for all women.

Sojourner Truth

In 1843 Isabella Baumfree was a free woman from New York who was once enslaved. She believed she had a duty to speak about ending slavery. Baumfree also believed that with her new life she had a new name. She began calling herself Sojourner Truth. Truth never learned to read because she was born into slavery and was not allowed to go to school. Still, she had good speaking skills and gave powerful speeches.

In 1849 an enslaved woman named Harriet Tubman ran away from her owner in Maryland and escaped to Pennsylvania. Tubman returned to the South nineteen times to help other enslaved people get to freedom.

Harriet Tubman was one of the most well-known "conductors" of the Underground Railroad. The Underground Railroad was not a railroad. It involved a group of people throughout the country. These people helped enslaved people escape from the South. They gave them safe places to stay on their journey. The Underground Railroad used railroad words to describe itself. The places where runaways would rest and eat were called stations and depots. They were run by stationmasters. People who donated money and supplies were stockholders. The conductors were in charge of moving runaways from one station to the next and **shielding** them from danger on the journey.

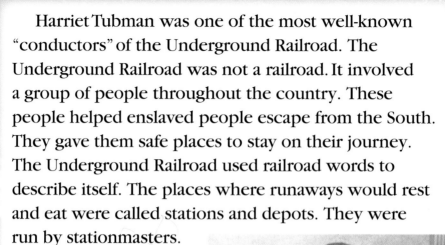

Harriet Tubman

President Abraham Lincoln signed the Emancipation Proclamation on January 1, 1863. This freed some enslaved people. But black people did not automatically get equal rights in the United States. In many areas they were not allowed to be in the same places as white people. Black people were separated from white people in schools, on buses, and in restaurants. It was not until the 1950s and 1960s that black people finally began getting equal treatment, but it was a struggle. This struggle to gain equal rights was known as the civil rights movement.

## The Civil Rights Movement

Until the early 1950s black children in some states were not allowed to attend school with white children. In 1952 some lawyers went to the U.S. Supreme Court, the highest court in the nation. They argued that black children should be able to attend school with white children. The lawyers said that separating black students from white students in schools based on skin color was unjust. They believed it should not be allowed. The Supreme Court agreed and made it illegal for black students to be prevented from going to school with white students.

Rosa Parks

Other changes were taking place in the 1950s. Black people were only allowed to sit in the back seats of buses: The front seats were for white people. In December 1955 a woman named Rosa Parks was arrested in Montgomery, Alabama, because she would not give up her seat on a bus to a white person.

When other black people heard about the arrest of Ms. Parks, they decided to boycott, or stop using, the buses. Then, in 1956, the U.S. Supreme Court ruled that separating people on buses was unconstitutional, against our country's basic principles.

The fight for equal rights continued into the 1960s. Black people were not allowed to eat at lunch counters or restaurants with white people. In 1960 four black students in North Carolina went into a store and sat down at the lunch counter. No one would serve them because they were black. The students stayed at the lunch counter until closing.

The next day, the students came back. They brought more students with them for support. Soon the idea caught on. Students in other cities started going to lunch counters and refusing to leave, even though they were never given any food.

The black students were sometimes badly treated by white people during this time. The students **avoided** using violence toward others, though. They chose to let their actions speak for themselves. Some students in North Carolina even formed their own group called the Student Nonviolent Coordinating Committee, or SNCC.

Black students sitting-in at a lunch counter in 1960

Black people finally made the United States see that they were not going to give up. They wanted their equal rights. They were not going to be separated from white people because of the color of their skin. On August 28, 1963, about 250,000 people, black and white, gathered for the March on Washington. They marched to the Lincoln Memorial in Washington, D.C. They came to ask President John F. Kennedy and Congress to give all people equal rights to education, jobs, and the use of public places. They had come together to let their voices be heard.

March on Washington

Reverend Dr. Martin Luther King, Jr.

A young **minister** named Reverend Dr. Martin Luther King, Jr., attended the March on Washington. He was a long-time leader in the civil rights movement. He helped lead the bus boycott in Montgomery, Alabama. Dr. King was a powerful speaker. He stood before the huge crowd of marchers in Washington, D.C., just as he stood at the **pulpit** of his church. He gave a speech called "I Have a Dream." Dr. King spoke of his hope that one day people of all backgrounds would be able to treat one another as equals. He believed in nonviolence, and he spoke with strength. His dream was the dream of all his supporters who cheered for him to share his dreams for America's future.

## Making a Difference

By 1965 the government had passed more laws that gave people rights in the United States. One of the most famous of these laws was the Voting Rights Act of 1965. This act made it illegal for states in the

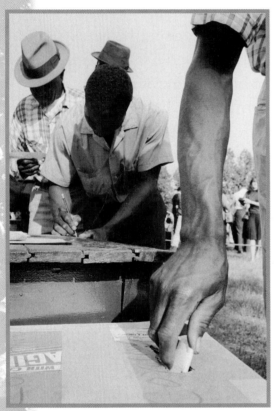

South to prevent black people from voting and letting their voices be heard on political decisions. As a result of the Voting Rights Act of 1965, the number of registered black voters grew. This law also helped many black people become a part of politics and get jobs in government.

Voting in Alabama

Integrated voting for the first time in a small town in Alabama

During the civil rights movement, African American people were known to sing a song that many of their **ancestors** had sung during the days of slavery. Bringing their voices together in song helped them to find strength. The song was called "We Shall Overcome." It was one of the many ways that African American people showed the United States that they would hold on until they were given equal rights.

Today there are still times when people across the United States struggle to be treated fairly. But they remember all the people in the past who refused to be treated differently because of the color of their skin, and they find the strength to overcome.

# Glossary

**ancestors** *n.* people from whom you are descended.

**avoided** *v.* kept away from.

**generations** *n.* people born about the same time.

**minister** *n.* member of the clergy; spiritual guide; pastor.

**numerous** *adj.* very many.

**pulpit** *n.* the platform or raised structure in a church from which the minister preaches.

**shielding** *v.* protecting; defending.